Bilingual Edition

Let's Draw with Shapes™

Edición bilingüe

Let's Draw a School Bus with Shapes

Vamos a dibujar un autobús escolar usando figuras

Joanne Randolph
Illustrations by Emily Muschinske

Traducción al español:
Mauricio Velázquez de León

The Rosen Publishing Group's
PowerStart Press™ & **Editorial Buenas Letras**™
New York

Published in 2005 by The Rosen Publishing Group, Inc.
29 East 21st Street, New York, NY 10010

First Edition

Book Design: Emily Muschinske

Photo Credits: p. 23 © Royalty-Free/CORBIS.

Library of Congress Cataloging-in-Publication Data

Randolph, Joanne.
Let's draw a school bus with shapes = Vamos a dibujar un autobús escolar usando figuras / Joanne Randolph ; illustrations by Emily Muschinske ; translated by Mauricio Velázquez de León.
p. cm. — (Let's draw with shapes = Vamos a dibujar con figuras)
Includes index.
ISBN 1-4042-7557-6 (library binding)
1. Motor vehicles in art—Juvenile literature. 2. Drawing—Technique—Juvenile literature. 3. School buses—Juvenile literature. I. Title: Vamos a dibujar un autobús escolar usando figuras. II. Muschinske, Emily, ill. III. Title. IV. Let's draw with shapes.

NC825.M64R36 2005
743'.8962922233—dc22

2004009907

Manufactured in the United States of America

Due to the changing nature of Internet links, PowerStart Press has developed an online list of Web sites related to the subject of this book. This site is updated regularly. Please use this link to access the list:
http://www.buenasletraslinks.com/ldwsh/autobus

Contents

Contenido

Draw a big red rectangle for the back of your school bus. Draw a small red rectangle for the front window.

Dibuja un rectángulo rojo grande para hacer la parte trasera del autobús. Agrega un rectángulo pequeño para dibujar la ventana delantera.

Add a long orange rectangle and two orange half circles for the top of your school bus.

Agrega un rectángulo largo y dos semicírculos de color anaranjado en la parte superior de tu autobús.

Draw a yellow rectangle and a yellow square for the front of your school bus.

Dibuja un rectángulo y un cuadrado de color amarillo en el frente de tu autobús escolar.

Add two green circles to make lights on your school bus.

Agrega dos círculos de color verde para hacer los faros de tu autobús.

Draw a blue circle and a blue half circle for the front wheels of your school bus.

Dibuja un círculo y un semicírculo de color azul para las ruedas delanteras de tu autobús escolar.

Add a purple circle and a purple half circle for the back wheels of your school bus.

Dibuja un círculo y un semicírculo de color violeta para las ruedas traseras de tu autobús escolar.

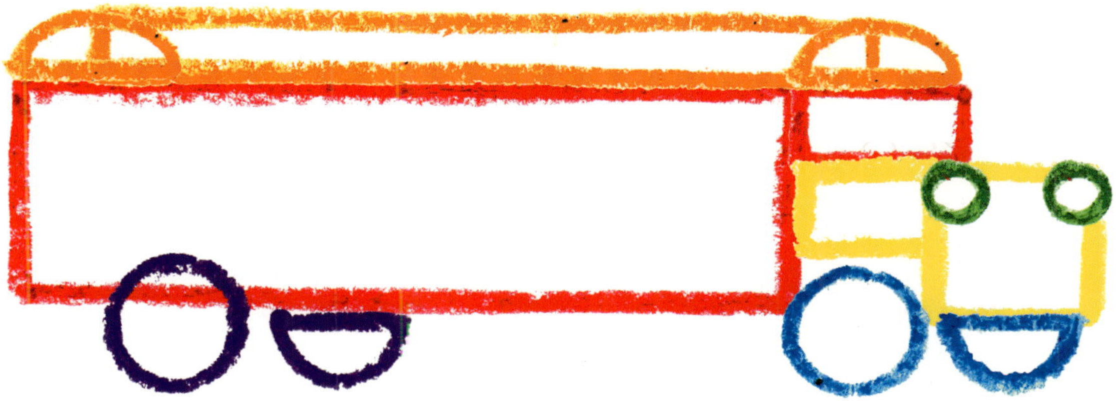

Draw seven pink rectangles for the windows on your school bus.

Dibuja siete rectángulos de color rosa para hacer las ventanas de tu autobús.

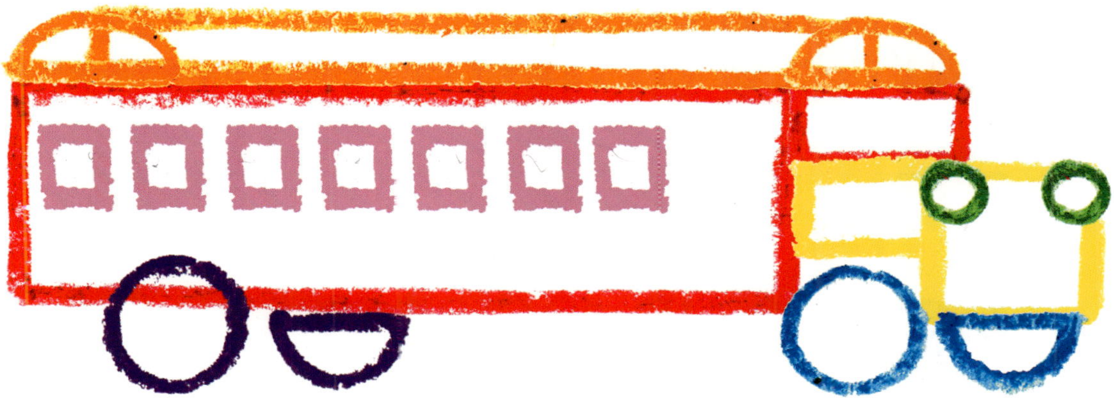

Add a black rectangle for the door of your school bus.

Agrega un rectángulo negro para la puerta de tu autobús escolar.

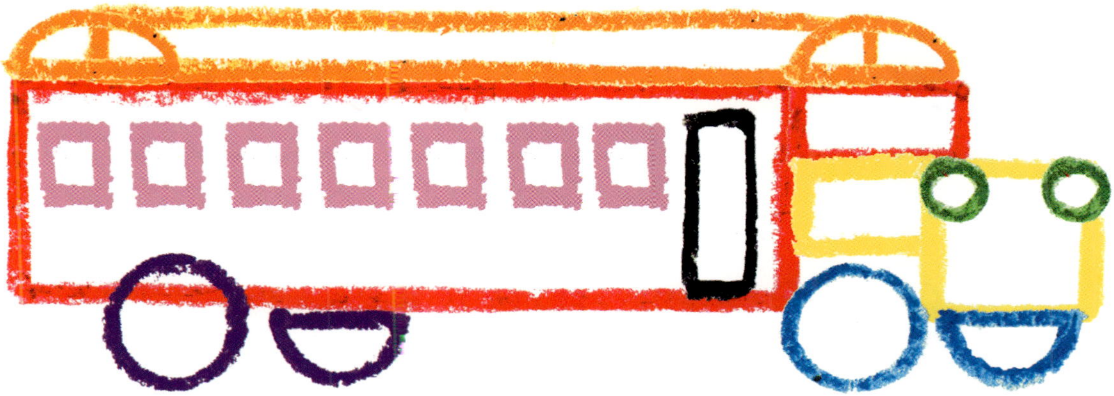

Color in your school bus.

Colorea tu autobús escolar.

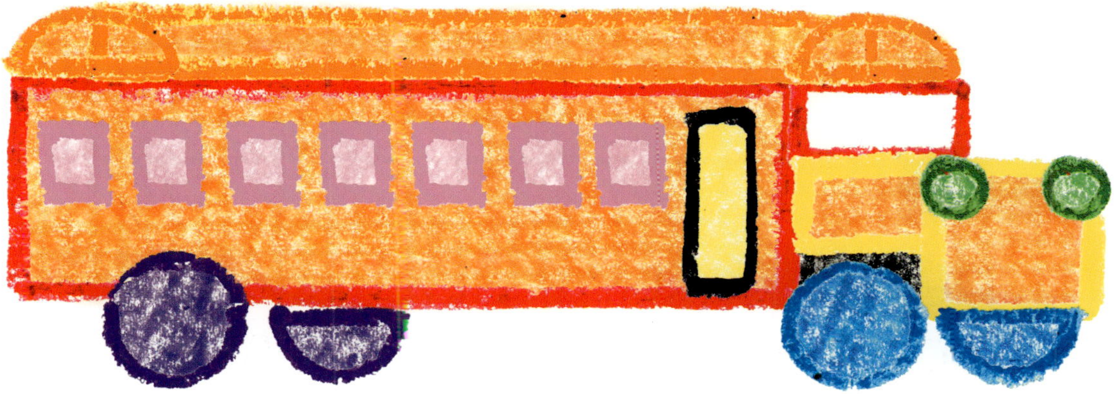

This school bus brings children to school each day.

Este autobús escolar lleva niños a la escuela todos los días.

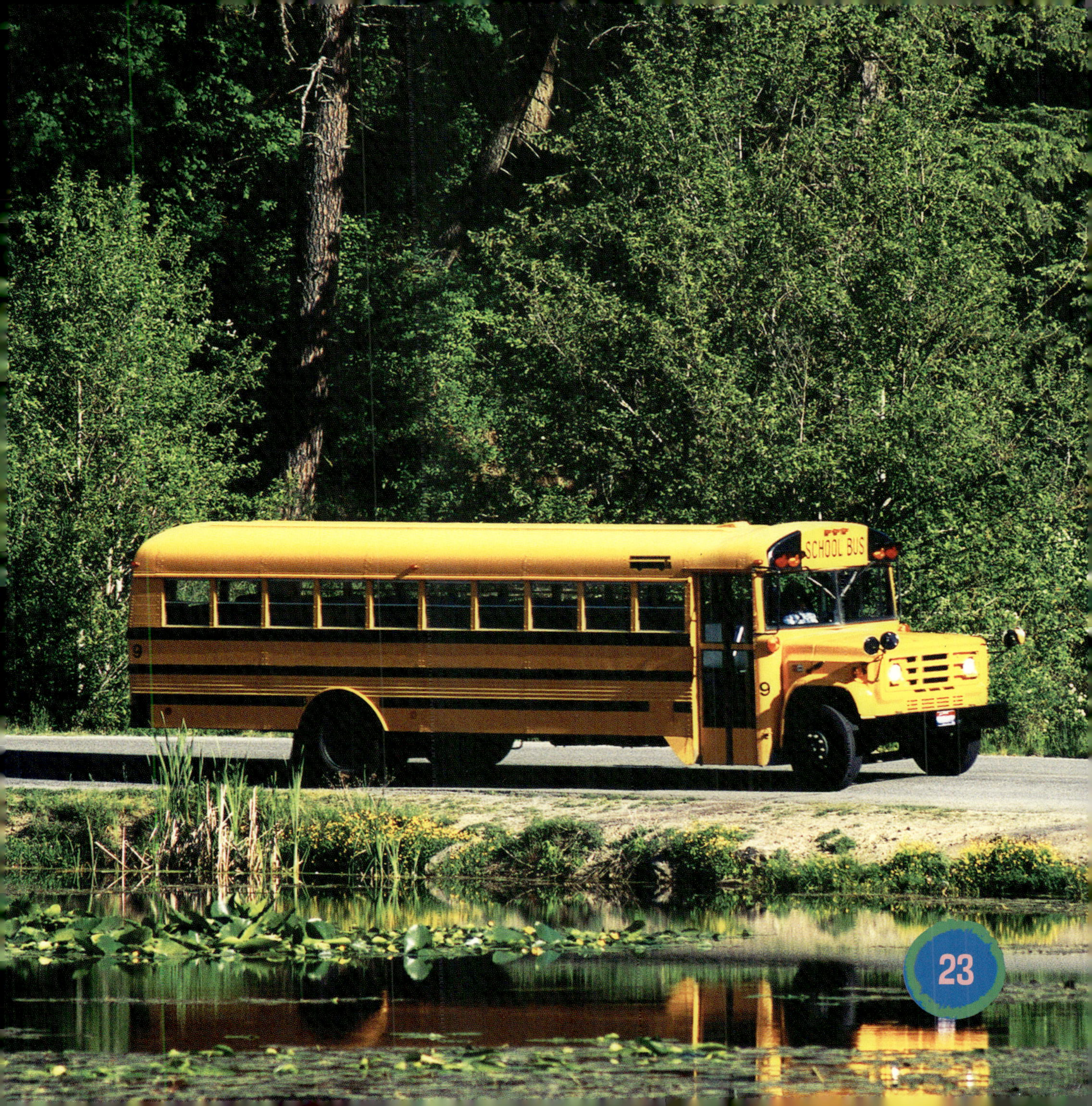
SCHOOL BUS

Words to Know/Palabras que debes saber

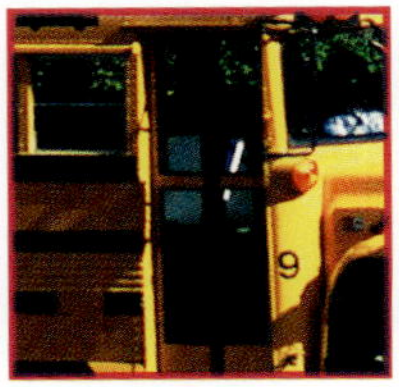

door/**puerta**

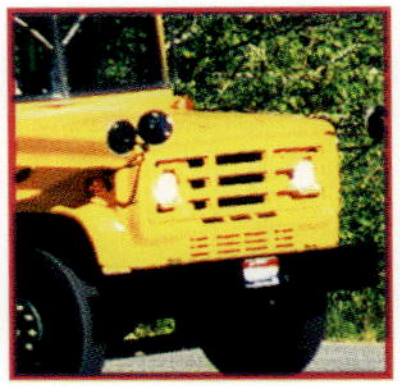

lights/**faros**

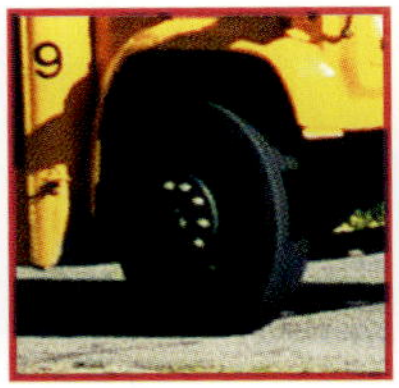

wheels/**ruedas**

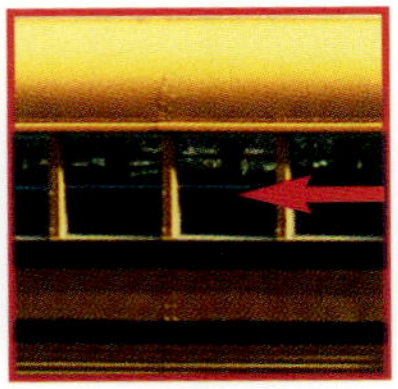

windows/**ventanas**

Colors/ Colores

red/**rojo**
orange/**anaranjado**
yellow/**amarillo**
green/**verde**
blue/**azul**
purple/**violeta**
pink/**rosa**
black/**negro**

Shapes/ Figuras

circle/**círculo**
square/**cuadrado**
triangle/**triángulo**
rectangle/**rectángulo**
oval/**óvalo**
half circle/**semicírculo**

Index

Índice